FRANCIS FRITH'S

# CLACTON-ON-SEA TOWN AND CITY MEMORIES

*Dad,*

*Merry Christmas,*

*Love,*

*Daniel.*

THE FRANCIS FRITH COLLECTION

www.francisfrith.com

FRANCIS FRITH'S
**TOWN** *&* **CITY**
MEMORIES

# CLACTON-ON-SEA

NORMAN JACOBS retired from the British Museum in 2005 after 37 years. He is founder and chairman of the Clacton & District Local History Society, and editor of the 'Clacton Chronicle'. He is the author of several books on the town and a well-known local speaker. He is the former chairman of Tendring District Council Leisure, Heritage & Culture Committee, and the former chairman of Museums in Essex Committee and Tendring Museums Forum. He is also a Trustee of the West Cliff Theatre.

DONKEY RIDES C1960 C107066

FRANCIS FRITH'S
# TOWN & CITY
MEMORIES

# CLACTON-ON-SEA

NORMAN JACOBS

FRANCIS FRITH'S
# TOWN & CITY
MEMORIES

First published as Clacton-on-Sea, A Photographic History of your Town
in 2001 by Black Horse Books, an imprint of The Francis Frith Collection
Revised edition published in the United Kingdom in 2006 by
The Francis Frith Collection as Clacton-on-Sea, Town and City Memories
Limited Hardback Edition ISBN 1-84589-144-9
Paperback Edition ISBN 1-84589-145-7

British Library Cataloguing in Publication Data

Clacton-on-Sea
Town and City Memories
Norman Jacobs

The Francis Frith Collection®
Frith's Barn, Teffont,
Salisbury, Wiltshire SP3 5QP
Tel: +44 (0) 1722 716 376
Email: info@francisfrith.co.uk
www.francisfrith.com

Aerial photographs reproduced under licence from Simmons Aerofilms Limited
Historical Ordnance Survey maps reproduced under licence from Homecheck.co.uk

Printed and bound in England

Front Cover: **CLACTON-ON-SEA, PIER AVENUE 1907** 58948t
The colour-tinting in this image is for illustrative purposes only,
and is not intended to be historically accurate

FRANCIS FRITH'S
# TOWN & CITY
MEMORIES

## CONTENTS

# THE MAKING OF AN ARCHIVE

Francis Frith, Victorian founder of the world-famous photographic archive, was a devout Quaker and a highly successful Victorian businessman. By 1860 he was already a multi-millionaire, having established and sold a wholesale grocery business in Liverpool. He had also made a series of pioneering photographic journeys to the Nile region. The images he returned with were the talk of London. An eminent modern historian has likened their impact on the population of the time to that on our own generation of the first photographs taken on the surface of the moon.

Frith had a passion for landscape, and was as equally inspired by the countryside of Britain as he was by the desert regions of the Nile. He resolved to set out on a new career and to use his skills with a camera. He established a business in Reigate as a specialist publisher of topographical photographs.

Frith lived in an era of immense and sometimes violent change. For the poor in the early part of Victoria's reign work was a drudge and the hours long, and ordinary people had precious little free time. Most had not travelled far beyond the boundaries of their own town or village. Mass tourism was in its infancy during the 1860s, but during the next decade the railway network and the establishment of Bank Holidays and half-Saturdays gradually made it possible for the working man and his family to enjoy holidays and to see a little more of the world. With characteristic business acumen, Francis Frith foresaw that these new tourists would enjoy having souvenirs to commemorate their days out. He began selling photo-souvenirs of seaside resorts and beauty spots, which the Victorian public pasted into treasured family albums.

Frith's aim was to photograph every town and village in Britain. For the next thirty years he travelled the country by train and by pony and trap, producing fine photographs of seaside resorts and beauty spots that were keenly bought by millions of Victorians.

## THE RISE OF FRITH & CO

Each photograph was taken with tourism in mind, the small team of Frith photographers concentrating on busy shopping streets, beaches, seafronts, picturesque lanes and villages. They also photographed buildings: the Victorian and Edwardian eras were times of huge building activity, and town halls, libraries, post offices, schools and technical colleges were springing up all over the country. They were invariably celebrated by a proud Victorian public, and photo souvenirs – visual records – published by F Frith & Co were sold in their hundreds of thousands. In addition, many new commercial buildings such as hotels, inns and pubs were photographed, often because their owners specifically commissioned Frith postcards or prints of them for re-sale or for publicity purposes.

In order to gain some understanding of the scale of Frith's business one only has to look at the catalogue issued by Frith & Co in 1886: it runs to some 670 pages. By 1890 Frith had created the greatest specialist photographic publishing company in the world, with over 2,000 stockists! The picture on the right shows the Frith & Co display board on the wall of the stockist at Ingleton in the Yorkshire Dales (left of window). Beautifully constructed with a mahogany frame and gilt inserts, it displayed a dozen scenes.

# THE MAKING OF AN ARCHIVE

## POSTCARD BONANZA

The ever-popular holiday postcard we know today took many years to appear, and F Frith & Co was in the vanguard of its development. Postcards became a hugely popular means of communication and sold in their millions. Frith's company took full advantage of this boom and soon became the major publisher of photographic view postcards.

Francis Frith died in 1898 at his villa in Cannes, his great project still growing. His sons Eustace and Cyril continued their father's monumental task, expanding the number of views offered to the public and recording more and more places in Britain, as the coasts and countryside were opened up to mass travel. The archive Frith created continued in business for another seventy years. By 1970 it contained over a third of a million pictures of 7,000 cities, towns and villages. The massive photographic record Frith has left to us stands as a living monument to a special and very remarkable man.

This book shows Clacton-on-Sea as it was photographed by this world-famous archive at various periods in its development over the past 150 years. Every photograph was taken for a specific commercial purpose, which explains why the selection may not show every aspect of the town landscape. However, the photographs, compiled from one of the world's most celebrated archives, provide an important and absorbing record of your town.

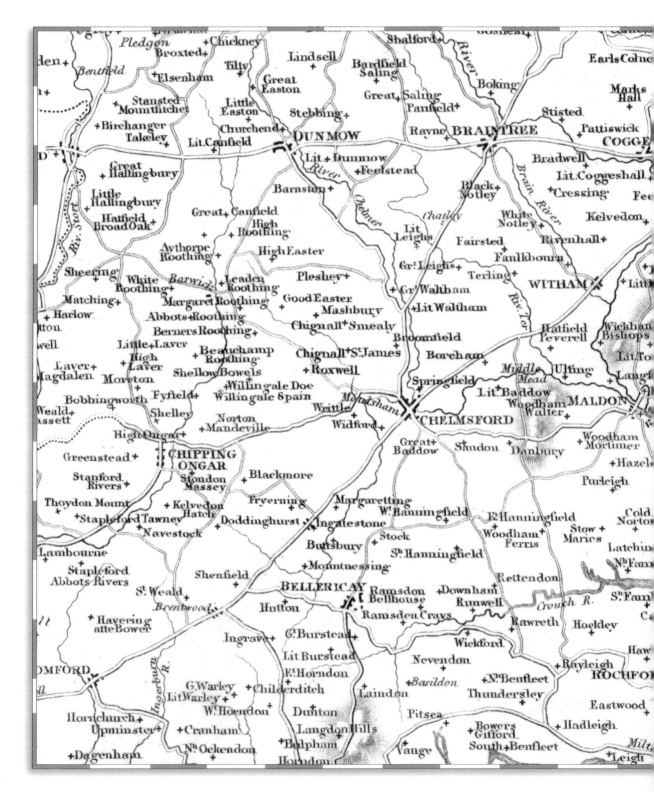

# ESSEX COUNTY MAP

A SECTION OF AN ESSEX COUNTY MAP c1850

(Notice Clacton-on-Sea does not appear by this date)

CLACTON-ON-SEA

> **BRABNER'S GAZETTEER 1895**
> There are good sands on either side of the pier, an esplanade below the cliff, and on the top a green serving as a ground for various sports.

# INTRODUCTION

BEFORE Queen Victoria came to the throne Clacton-on-Sea did not exist. What is now the centre of the town was a lonely desolate part of the Essex coast known as Clacton Beach after the village of Great Clacton situated about a mile or so inland.

It was not until 1864 that development began. In that year the land that was to become the centre of Clacton-on-Sea was put up for sale and was bought by a man called Peter Bruff, the engineer on the Colchester to Walton railway then being built. It was Bruff's intention to turn the area into a seaside resort as a speculative business venture and it is from this date that the real history of Clacton-on-Sea begins.

In 1866 Bruff was granted Parliamentary powers to construct a branch line from his railway to Clacton and to build a pier. The powers were granted for five years. By 1870 Bruff had done very little as his capital was tied up elsewhere. With just one year to go before permission lapsed, Bruff arranged a meeting with William Parry Jackson, the chairman of the Woolwich Steam Packet Company. In return for the rights to operate his company's steamers to and from the pier Jackson agreed to finance Bruff's scheme.

The first steamer to call at the pier was the 'Queen of the Orwell', which called in on its way to Ipswich on 18 July 1871, a date which could be said to be the birth of Clacton-on-Sea.

# INTRODUCTION

THE PIER 1907 58938

*The pier was the first building to be built in the new town of Clacton-on-Sea.*

# THE PIER

THE official opening of the pier came on 27 July 1871 when the SS 'Albert Edward' called, bringing with it a party of directors from the Woolwich Steam Packet Company and about 200 guests. At first the pier was built purely as a landing stage and was just 160 yards in length and four yards wide. A scale of charges was laid down for the landing of certain materials, including gunpowder at 6d; musical instruments, 1d per cubic foot; turtles 2s 6d and corpses £1 each. The toll for a walk along the Pier was 1d.

The first buildings on the pier were some weatherboard offices erected by the entrance and a shelter at the seaward end. The offices became the Pier Dining Rooms and then in 1885 the Hot and Cold Sea Water Baths, leased by the proprietor of the Royal Hotel opposite. In 1893 the first major alterations to the pier took place. It was widened and lengthened to 1,180 feet and a theatre, the Pier Pavilion, was built by architects Kinipple & Jaffrey at the sea end for the staging of 'Grand Concerts' (see 58937, page 14). During the Edwardian period and the 1920s the Pavilion became home to the White Coons, one of the leading concert parties of the time. It was later renamed the Jolly Roger and was used as the indoor base for the outdoor Rambla concert party, who put on their evening concerts there and also used it in wet weather.

THE PIER 1901 46692

*A close-up view of the Hot and Cold Sea Water Baths established by the Royal Hotel in 1885, gentlemen to the left, ladies to the right. At the end of the pier is the Pavilion, built in 1893. An advertisement at the entrance announces that a concert is 'now on'. To the right, mid way along, is a shooting saloon.*

# THE PIER

Above: FROM THE PIER 1914 66840

*A view from the pier showing some of the main features of
Clacton. From left to right can be seen the Blockhouses, the
Venetian Bridge, the Royal Hotel, the flagstaff, the Band
Pavilion and the old Town Hall clock.*

Right: THE PIER WITH A BELLE STEAMER 1907 58937

*By 1907 the Pavilion was under the proprietorship of
Harold Montague. At the entrance to the pier a small 'Ices
and Teas' kiosk has been added. One of the famous Belle
Steamers is approaching the pier.*

Before the pier was taken over by businessman Ernest Kingsman, there were still very few entertainments on the pier, just the Pavilion, now housing the White Coons, the shooting gallery and some jockey scales to the extreme left of the entrance (see 70263, left). The Baths had been converted into a small café, called The Cabin, on one side and a photographers, The Pier Studio, on the other.

During the First World War, the owners of the pier, the Coast Development Company, a successor company to the Woolwich Steam Packet Company, went into liquidation and was bought by Ernest Kingsman. Being a shrewd businessman he took the view that given the necessary capital and investment, together with determination and energy, Clacton Pier could become a big money spinner, but only by changing the whole concept of the pier.

He immediately set about turning the pier from what was still basically only a landing stage into the biggest pleasure pier in the country. To achieve this ambition he promoted a Private Bill in the House of Commons aimed at widening the front of the pier to 90 feet by the compulsory purchase of land owned by Clacton Urban District Council. The Bill was vehemently opposed by the Council but Kingsman was successful and able to continue his policy of building Clacton Pier into a major tourist attraction.

By the outbreak of the Second World War Kingsman had spent something like a quarter of a million pounds on building such attractions as the Ocean Theatre, the Children's Theatre, the Blue Lagoon Dance Hall, the Crystal Casino, the only open-air pier swimming pool anywhere in the country, the Steel Stella roller coaster and an open air concert party theatre. The pier was affectionately known as 'No 1 North Sea' and achieved Kingsman's ambition of becoming the biggest and one of the most frequently visited piers in the country.

During the war the pier was damaged by enemy action and was also breached to prevent its use by an invasion force. Two attractions, the Crystal Casino and the Children's Theatre, disappeared. Nevertheless, the 1950s saw Clacton Pier continue to hold its own as a major tourist attraction with new amusements being added such as the Helter Skelter, the Peter Pan Railway and the Ghost Train.

But the decline of Clacton as a major seaside resort in the 1960s, with more and more people going abroad for their holidays, also saw the decline of Clacton Pier, and in 1971 Barney Kingsman, Ernest's son, sold it. In 1973 the Steel Stella burnt down and in 1978 the Ocean Theatre closed. By 1980 practically all the major entertainments had closed although there were still a number of rides, such as the dodgems, as well as amusement arcades.

The pier has recently undergone a revival, but it is doubtful if the glory days of the 1920s, 30s and 50s will ever return.

# THE PIER

THE PIER 1921 70263

# THE PIER

THE CENTRAL PROMENADE c1936
C107007

*By 1936 Kingsman had spent about £200,000 on the pier and added many attractions such as Britain's first open air pier swimming pool (left), the Crystal Casino Amusement Arcade (centre), the Blue Lagoon Dance Hall (right) and the Ocean Theatre (behind the Blue Lagoon). To the left of this photograph, the Pier Studio had become Murray's Photographers and the Rambla Concert Party is being advertised.*

Above: THE BLUE LAGOON C1947  C107004

*The Blue Lagoon Dance Hall with dancing to Teddy Dobbs and his Orchestra was a favourite spot for Clacton's youngsters as well as visitors.*

Left: THE PIER APPROACH C1955  C107042

*A view looking across the Venetian Bridge to the pier, showing some later attractions, the Cresta Run Helter Skelter in the centre and, to the right, the Steel Stella rollercoaster, opened in 1938 and destroyed by fire in 1973.*

The Pier c1960  C107051

The Bridge 1919 69304

# THE TOWN CENTRE - BUILDINGS & DEVELOPMENT

LEADING up from the pier to the town itself a new ramp was cut in the cliff face and called Pier Gap. In 1887 shops were erected on both sides (see 64239, pages 24-25). These shops were designed for the holidaymaker and included such establishments as cafés, souvenir emporiums, shell fish shops and so on.

Photograph 64239 shows the shops which existed before the 'General Beautifying Programme' swept them away. Because of the steep slope the shops nearest the pier were larger and able to offer more goods. The shops included a bucket and spade shop; a fish and chip shop (1d the fish, ½d the chips); sweet shops selling Clacton rock; a beachwear shop (plimsolls 6½d a pair, paddling shoes 4½d); souvenir shops selling ashtrays, paperweights and snowstorms, all 'Presents from Clacton-on-Sea'; a postcard shop; a tobacconist (Woodbines five for a penny) and a sea-food shop.

By 1913 however, Clacton Council had become very concerned about the state of Pier Gap. It was becoming very dirty as it proved difficult to clean by the normal method of using a horse-drawn water cart because it was so steep. To remedy this the Council instituted what it called a 'General Beautifying Programme' and swept the shops away, replacing them with landscaped gardens and a bridge built to link the upper promenades. At the opening ceremony, which was performed by Alderman Colonel J Humphrey, the Sheriff of the City of London, the Mayor of West Ham congratulated the Council for carrying out the work by direct labour and for 'replacing the winkle and eel-pie shops previously down either side of the pier gap with beautiful flower beds and the bridge which stretched from cliff to cliff'.

PIER AVENUE 1921 70269

*Among the first houses to be built were three detached villas known as the Blockhouses, one of which can be seen on the left. These were built in 1874 at a total cost of £3,000. Their official name was Clarence Villas, but they soon acquired their irreverent nickname.*

Having built the pier, the next move by Peter Bruff and the directors of the Woolwich Steam Packet Company was to build a hotel. They formed a hotel company which, for £900, bought from Peter Bruff the street block to the east of the pier. Frederick Barnes of Ipswich was appointed architect and it was hoped to open the new hotel, to be called the Royal Hotel, in time for the 1872 season. The timetable was not met and although an official opening ceremony took place at the end of July, the first visitors were not accommodated until 17 August. The total cost of the building was £7,465. Because Bruff and the Woolwich Steam Packet Company controlled the town they placed a covenant on other premises which enabled the Royal to enjoy a virtual monopoly for a number of years both as a hotel and as a public house. During its first four months the bar took £377 and the hotel £535.

Within a year of building, a separate tap room was added at the rear. To attract trade outside the summer season the hotel advertised 'good Stabling and Horse Boxes for Hunters …. the Essex and Suffolk Foxhounds meet in the Neighbourhood within easy distance'.

Peter Bruff began to sell off other plots of land around Pier Avenue to individual developers, but he was determined that his town of Clacton-on-Sea should maintain proper standards. His vision of this new seaside resort was as a retreat for the upper middle classes and the generally better off.

To this end he laid down very strict conditions in his 'Deed of Mutual Covenants'. This dealt with draining, fencing, paving, lighting and other improvements 'maintaining and keeping for the common benefit and at the common expense the said New Sea side Town or Watering place called "Clacton-on-Sea"'. Peter Bruff was, to all intents and purposes, a one man Town Planning Committee. It is largely due to Bruff that the centre of Clacton still retains that airy and well laid out

# THE TOWN CENTRE - BUILDINGS & DEVELOPMENT

**Right:** PIER AVENUE C1960
C107052

*Leading up Pier Avenue from the Marine Parade corner, the first pair of houses on the left, known as Clarence Villas, was built in 1874. It was later converted into the Clarence Restaurant and a newspaper, office for Clacton's first newspaper the 'Clacton Gazette'. Between the wars the buildings became famous as the Corner House Café. They are now the site of a night club.*

**Below:**
THE ROYAL HOTEL 1891  28233

feel with wide streets and well-spaced shops and houses which remains to this day.

In 1877 the directors of the Woolwich Steam Packet Company, many of whom - such as Jackson, Ellis, Hayes, Penfold and Agate - are now remembered by roads named after them in the centre of town, together with James Harman as secretary, formed the Clacton-on-Sea General Land, Building and Investment Company Limited with a capital of £500,000. They bought up all the unsold plots of land from Bruff and set about developing Clacton. They had already formed a number of other companies to develop specific undertakings. For example, in 1875 they had formed the Clacton-on-Sea Gas and Water Company, while in 1877, as a result of their Clacton-on-Sea Hall and Library Company, they were able to open Clacton's Public Hall with its adjoining assembly rooms, library, reading and retiring rooms and shops.

The Public Hall, the prominent building on the right with its wrought iron colonnade and large arched centre (see photograph 58948, pages 30-31), cost £7,000 and was one of the main features of the town. By the time of this photograph it had ceased to be a Public Hall and instead belonged to Lewellen, ironmongers and cycle stores. To the right of the Hall is Henry Foyster's Restaurant, a prominent business in Clacton from the 1890s until the 1950s. Next to Foyster's is W Mann, chemist, and between Mann's and the Royal Hotel is Ubsdell's Library, stationers and fancy goods.

The Public Hall was destroyed by a fire in June 1939. The fire, generally known as the Lewellen's fire after the shop which had taken over the main part of the Hall, also destroyed a large part of Pier Avenue, from the Castle Restaurant at the north almost to the Royal Hotel at the south.

The most prominent buildings on the other side of Pier Avenue at the lower end were the Brunswick Hotel and the Royal Bazaar.

The Brunswick Hotel was built in the 1870s originally as Brunswick House, a boarding and day school for 'young gentlemen' which was run by F J Nunn, but it was soon converted into a hotel. At the time of view 28230 on page 32 it was owned by Arthur Swann and was noted for its 'beanfeasts'. In 1891 full board and lodging would have cost two guineas per week and a roast and two veg dinner, 1s 6d. In the 1930s the hotel and restaurant, seen in 28230 selling American Ices and Drinks, was

Left: THE ROYAL HOTEL 1913 65237

*The original building occupied less than half its present frontage and was extended eastwards in 1874. Two years later the bars fronting Pier Avenue were added. The remaining frontage, incorporating a dining hall, was completed in 1881.*

PIER AVENUE 1907 58948

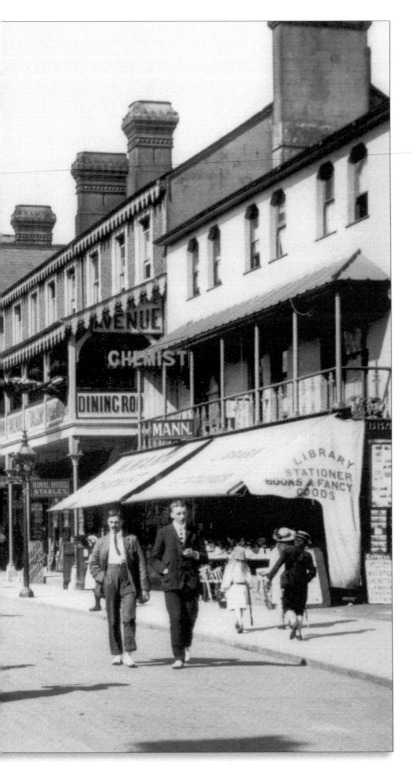

converted into an amusement arcade, known firstly as Brunswick Amusements and then as Marshall's Amusements. It is now home to Magic City.

Towards the end of the 19th century the Ainslie Brothers arrived in Clacton and opened a butcher shop in Station Road. The Ainslie Brothers had a string of shops in the South East and were looking to expand their business in other ways. At the turn of the century the London building firm of Ellis and Turner were building a whole parade of shops for the Ainslies in Surbiton and, when a piece of land became available in Clacton, the brothers decided to build a similar parade on it. They employed a London architect, A L Guy, to design the parade, which became known as Electric Parade as it was the first street in Clacton to be lit by electricity and was powered by two gas engines, two dynamo machines and a fine switchboard.

The 'Clacton News' of 29 June 1901 contained the advertisement on page 33.

The grand lighting up ceremony was performed on Tuesday 23 July 1901 and the whole parade was adorned with flags for the occasion. Only half the Parade was finished, but among the new premises opening was the town's first proper Post Office. The Ainslie Brothers themselves opened a second butcher shop in the Parade and it was in this shop, now the Meat Inn, that the electrical equipment was kept.

# The Town Centre - Buildings & Development

Right: ELECTRIC PARADE 1913 65239

*Electric Parade is on the left of this photograph. Some of the shops which can be seen include George Petley's Toilet Saloon; the cleaners, Achille Serre; Mrs Finch's confectionery shop and tea rooms; Turner, gentlemen's outfitters and A E Schulkins Electric Cigar Stores, selling Indian, Mexican and Havana cigars.*

Above: PIER AVENUE 1891 28230

*The Royal Bazaar was opened by Frederick Collins in the 1880s as the Royal Bazaar and Fancy Repository. Collins had another shop in Pier Gap. In the early 1920s the premises were converted into a restaurant, the Garrick, and then rebuilt to become a branch of the National Provincial Bank and later Lloyds Bank.*

Right: PIER AVENUE C1955 C107043

*With Lewellen's fire coming so close to the outbreak of war, the buildings were not replaced until the early 1950s when Baughan and Spalls took their place alongside older established businesses such as the Castle Restaurant and Foyster's Restaurant.*

By August 1902 all the shops had been let and a second opening ceremony was performed which fortunately coincided with King Edward VII's coronation so it provided another excuse to get out the bunting and Japanese lanterns. The Parade was crowded with visitors until midnight. Among the shops to open in 1902 was Ernest Newson's tailors.

The name Electric Parade was discontinued at the end of the 1950s at the request of the Post Office and the shops were renumbered as part of Pier Avenue. The service road at the back of the Parade is still known today as Back Electric Parade.

At the end of Electric Parade, Pier Avenue continued on until it met the ancient road – Old Road – from Great Clacton down to Clacton Beach. Just across from Electric Parade, on the corner with Rosemary Road, the Wesleyan Methodists built Trinity Church. Methodist congregations are recorded as far back as the 1790s in the village of Great Clacton and in 1824 they opened a chapel in Valley Road. The first recorded meetings in Clacton-on-Sea took place in 1875 when James Harman offered his lecture hall in Orwell Road as a meeting place on the spot where the Geisha Hotel stands today. Within two years the congregation had built their own church, the Trinity Methodist Church.

The other main road which, along with Pier Avenue and Rosemary Road, forms the centre of Clacton-on-Sea, was originally known as North Avenue, but after the coming of the railway in 1882 was renamed Station Road as it is the road leading directly to the station. On the small block between Pier Avenue and

# THE TOWN CENTRE - BUILDINGS & DEVELOPMENT

Pallister Road is the impressive Bank Building built in 1899 to house the London & County Bank as well as a number of shops, including the Home and Colonial Stores.

As Clacton-on-Sea grew the justification for an independent local authority also grew. At a special meeting held in September 1890 the town agreed to petition for the creation of a Local Board of Health, the forerunner of the local council. After an enquiry Essex County Council duly authorised the new Board which came into being as the Great Clacton Local Board on 17 June 1891. Its powers covered draining, lighting, paving, approval of new roads and buildings, sanitary inspection and powers to acquire and maintain parks and pleasure grounds.

STATION ROAD 1904 51537

*Bank Building, on the right, was designed by local architect T H Baker and constructed by the Colchester firm Everett & Son. The building cost £5,000 and included a spacious flat for the manager, Mr Wallace. Mr Baker, whose office was in Station Road, was responsible for designing a number of buildings in Clacton-on-Sea including St Osyth Road School and Christ Church. Across Pallister Road is the town's first sub post-office, opened by Shadrach Sparling in his baker shop in 1874. In 1882 the shop was taken over by W E Thorogood who also opened a Japanese Tea Rooms on the premises. The letters W E T can still be seen today, picked out in a mosaic pattern on the floor at the entrance of the shop. On the left-hand corner of Station Road and Pier Avenue is the outfitters, Grimwade and Clarke. Firstly as Clarke and then as Grimwade and Clarke, this shop occupied that corner for over 80 years from the turn of the century until 1984 when it was demolished to make way for the McDonald's Restaurant which now stands on the site. Dominating the Clacton skyline in the background, on the corner of Station Road and Rosemary Road, is the Town Hall clock.*

PIER AVENUE 1913 65238

*Opened on 14 August 1877, Trinity Methodist Church could accommodate 500 people. A schoolroom was added in 1887 and within a year 225 children were on the register. The school lasted until 1893 when St Osyth Road School was opened under the auspices of the School Board.*

THE TOWN HALL 1904 51538

MUNICIPAL BUILDINGS C1955 C107038

The inaugural meeting was held in the Public Hall in Pier Avenue on 12 August. In 1892 a company was formed for the purpose of providing a Town Hall. An architect, J Wallis Chapman, was appointed and building began the following year on a plot of land at the corner of Station Road and Rosemary Road. Costing about £12,000 it consisted of a bank on the ground floor with Council Offices above, and a theatre.

The Board was able to take possession in April 1894. At the same time there was a major redevelopment of local government as district councils came into being, and on 9 January 1895 the Clacton Urban District Council, under the chairmanship of Henry Finer, held its first meeting in the new building.

On the opposite corner of Station Road and Rosemary Road from the Town Hall is Frederick Wagstaff, tobacconist and cigar merchant (see 51538, left). The building had originally been known as Walbrook House and in the 1880s and 90s had housed a number of the pioneers' companies, including the Land Company, the Gas and Water Company, the Pier Company and the Steamboat Company. By the turn of the century, Wagstaff had moved in and remained until the 1930s. He was a prominent member of Clacton Council and was chairman in 1920 and 1933. The site is still known today as Wagstaff's corner. In May 1941 this whole area, including much of the Town Hall and Wagstaff's corner, was badly damaged in an air raid. The Town Clock was demolished.

The Council had to vacate the premises in 1923 and the offices transferred temporarily to some old army huts which had been provided in Station Road. In 1928 the Council decided to build a new Town Hall on a one acre site, formerly a potato field, purchased in 1922. A Town Hall Buildings Committee was set up under Clacton's first Labour Party councillor, Jack Shingfield. Sir Brumwell Thomas was appointed architect for the project. Thomas had already been responsible for a number of municipal buildings, including Belfast City Hall, Woolwich Town Hall and Stockport Town Hall. The builders were Messrs Edwin Winn and Company and the Clerk of Works, Mr Prebble. The foundation stone was laid on 16 October 1929 by Mr William Whitelaw, the Chairman of the London and North Eastern Railway Company. The grand opening ceremony took place at 12.30 pm on Tuesday 14 April 1931, performed by H R H Prince Arthur of Connaught KG. As well as Council Offices, the building comprised a 1,250 seat theatre and public hall, known as the Princes Theatre, and the town's Public Library.

All political parties in the Council had combined to support the building of the Town Hall. It was a fine, clean-cut neo-Georgian building with a giant centre portico and pediment that proclaimed Clacton's sense of purpose to the world. In many ways the building and the grand opening ceremony can be seen as the high point of Clacton-on-Sea's history. They displayed to the public the pride and confidence Clacton felt at this time.

Just 60 years after the town's foundation, Clacton-on-Sea had become a thriving community; the Council was not only responsible for the local government of the town but also controlled its gas, electricity and water supplies. Clacton had become one of the country's leading seaside resorts and was definitely in the top league along with places such as Brighton and Blackpool.

# FROM THE AIR

CLACTON-ON-SEA, THE PIER FROM THE AIR 1931   AF39135

# WEST OF THE PIER

STRANGELY enough, given that the most popular beach area in Clacton has for long been to the west of the pier, the early seaside developments took place on the east side. By 1891, as can be seen in 28227, right, there had been very little development to the west and not many visitors either.

The first work on sea defences on the west side came in the early 1890s following which the west side began to take over in popularity from the east side. The first beach entertainers were probably L'Art Minstrels, who set up a stand on the beach about 1892-3. They were followed by Braide and Partridge's Minstrels and then by Jack Holland's Concert Party. By the Edwardian period there were three entertainment stands set up, more or less permanently, on the beach. Photograph 58942 shows Claude North's Living and String Marionettes stand. Next to it, nearer the Pier, was the Yorkshire Pierrots stand.

The Yorkshire Pierrots arrived in Clacton in 1901 (see 64237A). They gave three shows a day, the first two in Pierrot costume and the last in full evening dress. They advertised their show as 'thoroughly refined'. It was a very precarious existence as their standard of living depended on Clacton living up to its 'Sunny Clacton' reputation. Originally they made their money by 'bottling' - while they were performing on stage one of their number

Top: FROM THE PIER 1891 28227

Above: THE PIER AND BEACH 1907 58942

Right: THE YORKSHIRE PIERROTS 1912 64237A

# WEST OF THE PIER

would go round collecting money in a bottle. Eventually they roped off part of the beach and charged admission to the enclosure, for which privilege they had to pay Clacton Council £4 rent per week, in advance. The Yorkshire Pierrots appeared every season from 1901 until 1912, when on 6 August an unusually high tide washed their stage out to sea. After that experience, they moved to an inland site!

As well as the beach entertainments a lot of other activities took place on the beach and there were many shops offering holiday makers a range of services.

Other facilities included the City and Suburban Jockey Scales in a kiosk to the right of the Yorkshire Pierrots and, of course, the bathing machines, owned by Alfred Cattermole. Bathing machines were provided so people could change into their bathing costume in private and then step straight into the sea. In those days it was not the done thing to change or sit around in bathing costumes on the beach.

Above: THE BEACH AND PIER 1904 51527
*From right to left there is Lipton's Tea shop; H Norman's ice cream and lemonade kiosk; Batty, the photographer, who periodically used to come out of his tent, blow a whistle and line people up for a group photograph which was available later in the day from his tent and shop in town; Baxfield's Fresh Oysters; Osborne, who sold 'the best cakes on the beach'; and J Rouse's tea shop.*

Far Left: KINGS PROMENADE FROM THE PIER 1912 64242
*The building on the right was built in 1899. Part of it was a pumping station used to pump sea water to standpipes dotted around the town for Council workmen to draw off water to wash down the dusty streets. Residents could also buy a key to enable them to bring relief to their tired feet.*

Left: THE BEACH 1904 51529

# WEST OF THE PIER

In the centre of photograph 51529 is a covered slope going up the cliff face. This is the Reno Electric Stairway. Opened in 1902 it was an escalator designed to 'convey passengers from Lower Promenade to Greensward' at the cost of 1d. It was operated by an electric motor and had a speed of 100 feet per minute. It was, however, a bit of a failure as people didn't see why they should pay 1d to travel up the cliff on an escalator when they could walk up the path for nothing. Consequently, in June 1906, the Reno Company wrote to the Council asking for permission to remove it. Finally in 1908 after much financial wrangling the Reno Company removed the machinery leaving the Council with the structure itself. On 3 February 1909, the Council resolved that 'The whole of the Reno structure be removed and that a sloping path be constructed' in its place.

THE PIER C1960 C107062

*Some entertainments did manage to survive the passing years, including the Punch and Judy show which was operated by Claude North's son, Claude North Junior. This lasted until well into the 1960s and in fact has recently been revived. Another popular entertainment over the years has been the many pleasure boats which have operated off the west beach, including the 'Viking Saga', the 'Jill', and the one in this picture, 'Nemo II'. The 'Nemo' began operations in 1928 and was bought by Dick Harman in the early 1950s. He continued to run it until 1982.*

# WEST OF THE PIER

Right: THE BEACH c1950 C107037

*Although the beach parties and other facilities disappeared over the years, the west beach remained very popular - as this photograph from c1950 shows. It used to be said that at times there were so many people on Clacton's beach the tide could not get in!*

Above: THE BEACH c1955 C107040

# WEST OF THE PIER

THE GARDEN OF REMEMBRANCE c1960 C107050

Above and Detail Below:

THE GLENGARIFF HOTEL C1955 C107015

*A tranquil scene at another of Clacton's hotels.*

Left: THE WAVERLEY HOTEL 1913 65236

With the Reno Electric Stairway no longer in operation, the way up from the beach to the Marine Parade and the attractive gardens is via one of the many paths cut into the cliffs (see C107040, page 46). The flower gardens to the west of the pier came about as a result of the Council filling in the clifftop trenches dug as a precautionary measure in the First World War. The idea of a Garden of Remembrance and War Memorial was first mooted at a public meeting held in 1918. A committee of 90 people was elected to progress the matter. In 1919 Mr C L Hartwell ARA presented his design for the monument, which was a picturesque study of the Spirit of Glory (see C107050, pages 48-49). In 1923 work commenced on its erection on a spot in the Garden of Remembrance, which had been the site of the armistice memorial service for the previous three years. Mrs R W Coan performed the ceremony, during which she deposited a casket containing the records of the town in the base of the pedestal. The memorial was unveiled on 6 April 1924 by the Rt Hon Lord Lambourne, the Lord Lieutenant of Essex, and was dedicated by the Bishop of Colchester.

Overlooking the Gardens and the sea, many hotels were built along Marine Parade East. The Waverley (see 65236, left), however, started life as The College, a boys' school, opened by Messrs Nunn and Crouch in 1881. In its early days Clacton-on-Sea was very popular as a location for private schools. The health-giving properties of its bracing sea air were said to aid education. Others included the Brunswick, Ascham College, Lansdowne House and Bedford Collegiate School for Girls. The College lasted for about ten years, after which it was converted into a hotel called the Waverley which still exists as one of the main hotels in Clacton, now renamed Days Inn.

A major contribution to the entertainments provided by Clacton-on-Sea came about in 1906 with the opening of the Palace-by-the-Sea by the playwright and author, G R Sims (see 58947 and 64260, pages 52-53 and 54). It contained a large galleried theatre complete with lounge and buffet. The theatre, long since closed, was demolished in the 1970s with the rest of the site being cleared in the early 80s. Clacton Hospital was extended over the site.

At the rear of the Palace there were extensive pleasure grounds modelled on the many Earl's Court exhibitions then in vogue, such

# WEST OF THE PIER

The Palace 1907  58947

# WEST OF THE PIER

Above and Detail Below:
THE BEACH, WEST END 1907 58943

Left: THE PALACE 1912 64260

as the Franco-British Exhibition. Among other attractions the grounds contained a bandstand, a skating rink, the Madeira Promenade, Illuminated Electric Fountains, the Blue Caves of Capri, a Neapolitan Pergola, a Tibet Pavilion and a Japanese Pagoda. Unfortunately, the upkeep for all this was enormous and, although the Palace-by-the-Sea was a popular attraction, the owner very soon went bankrupt and the pleasure grounds were closed, leaving just the Theatre to operate on its own. In 1922 a Birmingham repertory company performed a Welsh comedy called 'The Barber and the Cow' in the theatre. Three members of the cast were Cedric Hardwicke, Ralph Richardson and Laurence Olivier. The theatre was eventually converted into a cinema. After the Second World War a small amusement arcade and pub opened on the site.

At the far west end of the beach a smaller version of the pier, known as the jetty, was built in 1898 (see 58943, left). This was to allow barges to unload the building materials necessary for the development of the new town of Clacton-on-Sea but, like the Reno Electric Stairway, it was a complete failure as the barge owners did not see why they should pay to unload on the jetty when they could just run up on to the beach, unload, wait for high tide and float off for nothing. Between the wars the jetty imitated its big brother by providing entertainments such as Harry Frewin's Jolly Coons and various other amusements. It was destroyed at the beginning of the Second World War as a precautionary measure.

To the right in photograph 64255, pages 58-59, is the concert party stand of Harry Frewin's Jolly Coons. Frewin had originally been a member of the Yorkshire Pierrots but left in 1907 to form his own company, the White Coons. They were forced to change their name when Will Pepper's White Coons, an older established troupe, turned up in Clacton to appear on the pier. In spite of being a little out of the centre they were very popular and the 'Clacton Graphic' reported in 1914: 'The Jolly Coons are going great guns at the Jetty Promenade and are well supported by visitors to the town'. After the First World War they appeared on the jetty for several seasons.

# WEST OF THE PIER

FROM THE JETTY 1912 64252

# WEST OF THE PIER

Above: DONKEY RIDES C1960 C107066

*Clacton's donkeys are seen here taking children for a ride in 1960 as they had done for over 75 years. The first operator was licensed in 1886, with the last going out of business in 1997. In the background is an Eastern National open top bus, used in the summer only for journeys along the sea front.*

Left: ON THE SANDS 1912 64255

# WEST OF THE PIER

WEST BEACH 1912 64254

*This photograph shows how the barges unloaded their cargoes which were mostly bricks, sand, cement, slate, timber and flint. The cargo was unloaded between high tides. While straightforward in mild weather it could be a bit tricky if the weather turned rough. The three horses used for pulling the carts up the beach can be seen in the picture. They took them as far as Wash Lane from where they were distributed to the various builders' yards around Clacton. The jetty beach also provided some of the necessary accoutrements for a seaside holiday such as bathing machines and deck chair hire (see 64252 on pages 56-57).*

# WEST OF THE PIER

In 1936 Billy Butlin arrived in Clacton. He bought an area of land at the west end of the promenade known as the West Clacton Estate. As well as the jetty, the estate comprised five cafés, two boating lakes, four miniature golf courses, three large car parks, a mile of sea front with foreshore rights, numerous beach huts and, curiously, 15 of Clacton-on-Sea's golf club's 18 holes. Billy Butlin set about building a holiday camp and amusement park on the site. The amusement park opened in 1937 and the holiday camp in 1938. Catering originally for 1,000 campers it eventually grew to accommodate 6,000.

There was much controversy when Butlin's plans were originally announced, but the camp became such an integral part of the life of the town that it was seen as nothing short of a disaster when Butlin's eventually closed in 1983. It was not just the economic boost given by the holidaymakers that Butlin's brought to Clacton, but it was also the town's major employer: although mostly seasonal there was also a large number of permanent jobs. As well as direct employment Butlin's also provided much indirect employment as the camp used local services, such as the farms to supply the food and laundries to clean the linen. An attempt was made to keep the site going as a holiday centre, but the successors, Atlas Park, only stayed open for one year. The site is now a housing estate known as Martello Bay.

The last attraction to the west of Clacton is the airfield, opened in 1958 as a replacement for the airfield in Alton Park which had ceased to operate at the time of the Second World War. At one time, in the 1930s, Hillman Airways had operated a daily service from Clacton to Romford from the Alton Park airfield. However, the West Clacton airfield operated, and still operates, mainly pleasure flights.

Above: BUTLIN'S CAMP C1960 C107063

Right: THE AIRFIELD C1960 C107079

*This view from one of West Clacton's aeroplanes clearly shows the latest stage in Clacton's development as a seaside resort. With Butlin's closing and with many of the hotels and boarding and guest houses also closing, the most popular form of accommodation in Clacton became the caravan park, of which there are many dotted around Clacton, some, like Highfields, still growing in size.*

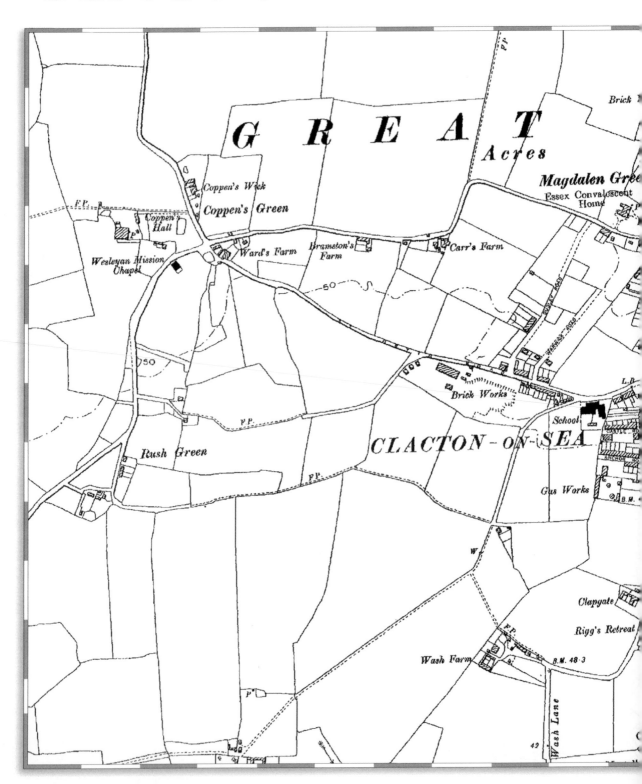

AN ORDNANCE SURVEY MAP SHOWING CLACTON-ON-SEA
AND SURROUNDING AREAS 1896

# EAST OF THE PIER

THE Sea Defence Commission was set up in 1880 with powers to provide protective works for the 'whole of the cliffs within the Clacton-on-Sea Special Drainage District, extending from Tower Road to Connaught Gardens'. It lost little time in beginning its work starting with the east side of the pier. By September 1881 a concrete wall extending from the pier as far as Vista Road had been completed (see 28226, below right). This gave the necessary protection and also provided a lower promenade.

Along the Marine Parade, horse-drawn hackney carriages waited to convey visitors around the town (see 58934, right). These were a popular form of transport until the 1960s, by which time they had faded away. A further licence was issued in 1981, but the revival did not last long. Between the carriages and the pier was Clacton's flagstaff. This was erected by the original Clacton-on-Sea Land Company and remained until the Pavilion was expanded in the late 1990s. Behind the second hackney carriage (see 58934) a man is watching the band from his bath chair. Bath chairs could be hired from Collin's Bazaar in Pier Gap.

The bandstand was built on the upper promenade in 1899. Clacton had formed its first band committee in 1887 and engaged the services of one George Badger as bandmaster. His job was to provide a band of ten 'thoroughly good and efficient musicians all dressed in uniform'. The band was to play for at least seven hours a day and the weekly wage was £10 per week to share between himself and the ten musicians. Some collections were also permitted. At first it had to play at various sites around the town, but when the bandstand was built they were able to settle down. Guest army regimental bands also played during the summer season.

# CLACTON-ON-SEA

## EAST OF THE PIER

Above: THE BANDSTAND AND PIER 1907 58934

Left: FROM THE PIER 1891 28226

# EAST OF THE PIER

THE BANDSTAND 1907 58935

*During the Edwardian period the area round the bandstand proved very popular for sitting out enjoying the sun or for strolling along the promenade.*

# EAST OF THE PIER

# EAST OF THE PIER

THE BAND PAVILION 1914  66844

# EAST OF THE PIER

As part of the General Beautifying Programme which swept away the shops in Pier Gap and erected the Venetian Bridge, a new home was also found for the Bandstand as a new glass-fronted Pavilion was erected to protect audiences from the wind.

The flat-roofed building on the right of 51532, pages 74-75, was originally built as a public hall by James Harman and was used by the Wesleyan Methodists before Trinity Church was built. The hall also served as lecture rooms, telegraph office and bank. It was later used by Harman's son, Clement, as a furniture warehouse and then, by the time of this photograph, it had passed to another son, John H, for use as auction rooms and an estate office. Later still the Geisha Tea Rooms were opened on the site and then the Geisha Hotel and Restaurant.

### THE BAND PAVILION 1914 66847

*This photograph was probably taken at the time of the opening ceremony of the Band Pavilion performed on 27 May 1914 by the Sheriff of the City of London. The bandstand was completely rebuilt again in 1936, when the old structure was done away with and a new stage built inside the Pavilion. After the Second World War the Pavilion became a very popular entertainment venue and attracted some of the leading big bands in the world, including Ray Connif, Ted Heath and Mantovani. It was also the home of resident bandmaster Ronnie Mills, one of the most popular entertainers in Clacton during the 1950s and 60s. The Pavilion played host to events such as the Ideal Holiday Girl Contest and the Evening Standard Fashion Show. It could accommodate audiences of up to three thousand.*

# EAST OF THE PIER

Above: THE GROSVENOR COURT HOTEL 1951 C107301 (DETAIL)

Right: THE PARADE 1904 51532

Below Left: THE TOWERS HOTEL 1893 31858A

Below Centre: GRAND HOTEL 1912 64251

Below Right: THE TOWERS AND GRAND HOTEL 1904 51535

As on the west side of the pier, the east side contained many hotels; in fact the hotels there were usually bigger than those on the west side. The Grosvenor Court, in C107301, left, for example, was a 3-star hotel accommodating 150 guests.

During the first 35 years of Clacton's existence the Sea Defence Commissioners continued their work tirelessly. After completing the work to the immediate east and west of the pier, their next move was to extend the sea wall beyond Vista Road with timber piling which was later replaced by a concrete wall. Below Vista Road there used to stand a plaque which read: 'This sea defence erected by the Clacton-on-Sea Commissioners was commenced July 1899 and completed March 1901'. The Commission was finally wound up in 1906 and its work transferred to Clacton Urban District Council.

The Towers Hotel, on the left in 31858A, left, was built in 1891. It stood in one and a quarter acres of its own grounds and catered for 150 guests in 90 bedrooms. It was the original home of Clacton Golf Club and provided two grass tennis courts, a nine-hole putting course, two croquet lawns, a bowling green and a full-size Burroughs and Watts billiard table. The Towers owned extensive property elsewhere, including Weeley Woods, which allowed its patrons the opportunity to go shooting in season, as well as its own farm which supplied all the food for its 'well-ventilated dining room'. By the Edwardian period the hotel was also able to cater for the motorist with a garage accommodating six cars. In a brochure issued by the proprietors, it was esteemed 'a favour if visitors will make any complaint - if cause should arise - direct to the Proprietors; where so much necessarily depends on servants, even with the most careful supervision, irregularities may arise'.

Clacton's biggest hotel was the Grand (see 64251 and 51535, left), built in 1897. During its day it eclipsed the Royal as Clacton's leading hotel and was the town's only AA and RAC four star hotel. It catered very much for the 'up-market' visitor and accommodated, amongst others, Prince Francis of Teck (Queen Mary's brother), Arnold Bennett and leading London theatre personalities such as Seymour Hicks and Ellaline Terriss. During the First World War it was the scene of a lunch provided by General Sir Arthur Paget for King George V, the only time a reigning monarch has ever visited Clacton-on-Sea. The Grand's cuisine was under the control of a Parisian chef and the main rooms were decorated with rich tapestries, Indian silks and rare embroideries. A 'famous band of lady minstrels, all trained musicians from the Royal Academy', performed daily in the drawing room. As the Grand's brochure said: 'Their rendering of classical pieces, as well as their singing of gipsy love songs and quaint old romances, constitutes a delightful feature in the daily programme'. Their brochure also noted that the hotel had 'filled a vital want in the resources of Clacton-on-Sea, having made this charming resort available for visitors of the best social position'.

The east side of Clacton, for many years known as Southcliff, provided a more gentle holiday than the west side. There were no concert parties or kiosks on the beach. No donkey rides or pleasure grounds. It was just the promenade for a quiet stroll. The hotels were generally larger than in other parts of town, the Grosvenor Court, the Towers and the Grand certainly, but also the Oulton Hall and the Hadleigh. The change that came over Clacton after the Second World War was reflected very much in what happened to the hotels. The Grand closed on the outbreak of war and opened briefly afterwards but closed down in 1949 and was taken over by the St Osyth's Teacher Training College. The 'East Essex Gazette' for 30 September 1949 noted that 'For one of the best sites on the Marine Parade to be occupied by a training college is an economic disaster'. But it was not the only hotel to become part of the St Osyth Training College. Next door the Towers, which never reopened at all after the war, also became part of the college. Later the Hadleigh and the Oulton Hall, whose advertising slogan was 'Where holidays are jolidays', were also incorporated into the college.

By the late 1960s there were very few large hotels left in the town and Clacton became a different sort of holiday resort, with Butlin's and the caravan camps catering for a younger clientele and eventually more for the day tripper or weekend visitor rather than the one week family holiday, which is how it largely remains today.

## PASSMORE EDWARDS HOME 1901 46693

*The Passmore Edwards Convalescent Home stood at the far end of the Promenade. It was conceived by John Passmore Edwards as a holiday home for deprived children. The foundation stone was laid by Sir H H Fowler MP on 19 May 1898 and the building officially opened on 23 June 1899. It eventually became a convalescent home and medical rehabilitation centre for the North East Metropolitan Region and was closed and demolished in 1986.*

# PAGE'S ESTATE

WHILE building was beginning on Bruff's original area of land at the centre of Clacton-on-Sea, another small estate was planned to the east beyond Beach Road and centred on Anglefield. The land had been bought by a local farmer and landowner, H J Page of Thorrowgood Farm, from the trustees of Charles Gray Round. Entitled the Cliff Estate, the land was offered for sale by auction in 33 lots which had been laid out by G Gard Pye, an architect and surveyor from Colchester.

The sale was carried out by auctioneers Sexton and Grimwade. While not part of Bruff's original scheme, the Cliff Estate did reflect his influence in the provisions for drainage - with the vendors guaranteeing to 'place a pipe drain along the back roads, with a junction, to which the

An Aerial View of Anglefield 1951 C107301

# PAGE'S ESTATE

purchaser of each lot could connect to the drains' - and in the restriction on the types of houses to be built, that is that in lots 1 to 7 and 29 to 33, no dwelling house was to be built of less value than £300, lots 8 to 28, no detached house of less than £400, or pair of semi-detached houses of less value than £700. The auction took place in June 1872 but only 18 of the plots were sold. The unsold lots were again offered for sale in 1873.

Shortly afterwards a conflict arose between the two main landowners, Bruff and Page, over the siting of a new church for Clacton-on-Sea, and a committee was set up to consider the matter. Bruff offered some land plus £100 towards the erection of the church and Page, supported by James Harman, also offered land, with Harman offering to become 'responsible for the larger share of the necessary funds'. When the committee accepted Page's offer, Bruff withdrew from it. The foundation stone was laid by James Round MP in 1874 and the church, named St Paul's, was opened in 1875 and became a parish in its own right in 1878. It was one of the first buildings erected on Mr Page's latest plot of land and for many years it stood quite alone in the fields. Ironically, in 1890 a mission hall was erected in High Street because it was felt that St Paul's was too far from the centre of town.

Over the next two years Page continued to lay out most of his farm as far as Victoria Road for development. For many years the gap in the cliff leading from the end of Victoria Road down to the Marine Parade remained the eastern limit of Clacton-on-Sea. At this time there were about 50 houses in the town.

St Paul's Church (see 28235, pages 82-83) cost £1,050 to build. However it soon proved too small for the growing town and a chancel, transepts, vestry, brick organ chamber and additional seating were added and the enlarged building was consecrated in 1881 by the Bishop of St Alban's. Damage was caused during the war, when a V2 rocket destroyed part of the roof, ceilings,

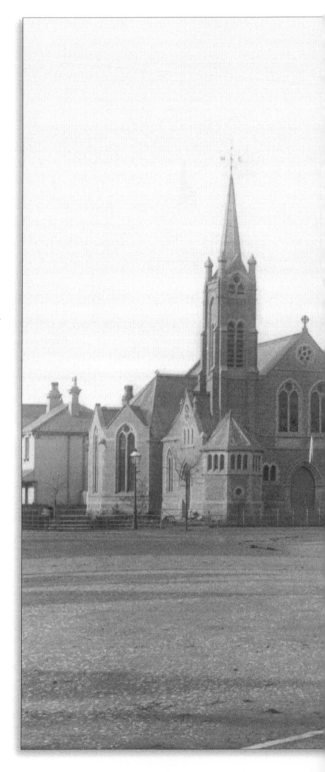

CHRIST CHURCH 1891 28234

*To the right, behind the flagpole is the Life Boat House, designed by Charles H Cooke and opened in 1878. The building was enclosed by a fence to protect it from damage by cattle. The round dormer window at the top admitted light to the roof space which housed two large hooks for raising and lowering the boat on to its carriage. A winding staircase led up the tower to the left where a warning bell was hung to summon the crew when needed. The boat was then drawn down to the beach by horses and launched from the beach.*

# PAGE'S ESTATE

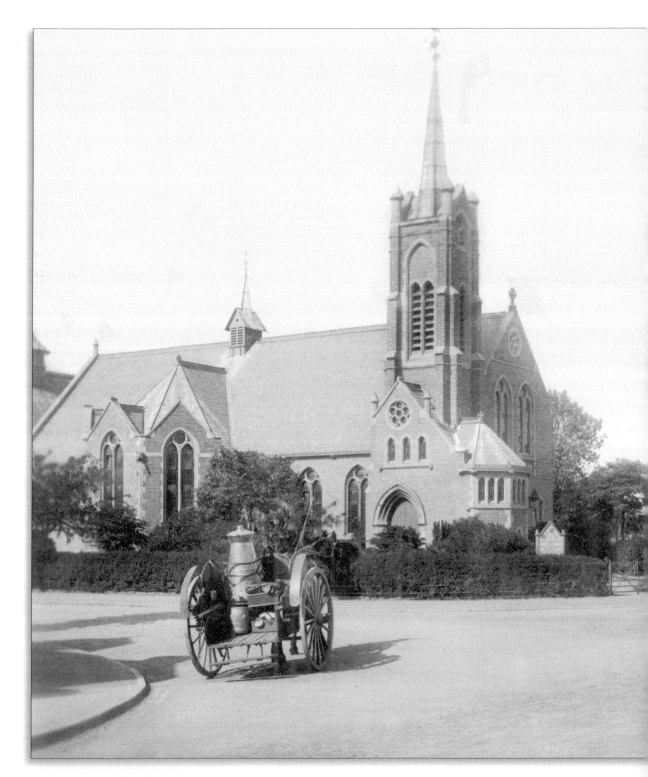

walls and windows. Planning permission was eventually obtained in March 1962 for repairs and enlargement, followed in August 1964 by permission to demolish the church altogether and build a completely new one. In June 1965 demolition began and the new church started. Consecration of the new St Paul's took place on 15 July 1966 and the final demolition of the old church completed shortly afterwards.

Clacton's next church, after St Paul's and Trinity Methodist Church, was built on Anglefield itself. It came about largely as the result of the work put in by two Colchester ministers, the Rev Thomas Batty of the former Stockwell Congregational Church and the Rev Edward Spurrier of Eld Lane Baptist Church. In 1885 a plot of land at the back of Anglefield, on the corner of Carnarvon and Holland Roads, was secured for £375 and designs for a new building were invited. The successful architect was local man, Thomas Baker. The building, in Early English Gothic style, was opened on 29 June 1887 at a cost of £2,040.

As well as many private schools the bracing air led to a number of convalescent and children's homes being built in Clacton. These included the Essex Convalescent Home at Magdalen Green, the John Groom Crippleage and Orphanage, Crossley House, Reckitt's, St Michael's and the Ogilvie School of Recovery, but the biggest of them all was the Middlesex Convalescent Home.

THE CONGREGATIONAL AND CATHOLIC CHURCHES
1904 51539

*To the right of Christ Church is the Catholic Church of Our Lady of Light. The architect was F W Tasker and the church was opened on 15 October 1903. It is cruciform in plan and consists of a nave of five bays with transepts to the north and south.*

# PAGE'S ESTATE

Building started on the Middlesex Convalescent Home in 1894 (see 64256 on pages 84-85) and it was officially opened on 1 July 1896 by the Duke and Duchess of York, the future King George V and Queen Mary, not with a celebration in Clacton, but with a special fete at the Middlesex Hospital in London.

For a number of years the five acre site stood in splendid isolation with magnificent views of the sea across open fields which had formerly been Clacton's first golf course and was later to become the Gardens area. The home had cost £30,000 to build and was designed to accommodate 26 men, 17 women and 12 children. An annexe for consumptive patients was subsequently added. The home's most notable role however was to accommodate wounded soldiers throughout the First World War. Shortly after the Second World War the home was transferred to the Kensington and Chelsea Health Authority and it was closed by them in 1977. It was subsequently taken over by the North East Essex Health Authority and was used to accommodate up to 70 mentally handicapped patients and as a small day care unit. It was finally closed in 1985 and the site was acquired by Wimpey Homes. The building still stands and is given over to private dwellings.

Eventually Page's Estate, Bruff's Estate, together with other estates around Clacton such as Round's Estate and Burrsville, linked up with the ancient villages of Great Clacton and Magdalen Green as well as the outlying areas of Jaywick and Little Holland, to form what we know today as Clacton-on-Sea.

Maybe its glory days of the 1920s and 1930s are gone, but with its several miles of golden sand, its gardens and its entertainments and amusements Clacton-on-Sea still has much to offer to the holidaymaker and resident alike.

ST PAUL'S CHURCH 1891  28235

# PAGE'S ESTATE

# PAGE'S ESTATE

THE MIDDLESEX CONVALESCENT HOME 1912 64256

# NAMES OF SUBSCRIBERS

The following people have kindly supported this book by purchasing limited edition copies prior to publication.

Peter Bailey

Mr and Mrs Ruth and Frank Baker

To Gran, Alex and the Basticks, loved and lost

Nancy Bastick

Alex Bastick

Peter A Beeney

Dear Bernard, happy memories, Joan

Alfred and Olive Berry, 2006

In memory of Lorna Mary Bradd

To Pam and John Brett

G W J Brown

The Bull family, love Joan

Ron Cartland, on his 65th birthday

Remembering Charlie, Sally, Fred, Diane,
    Alex and Tilly

Mr and Mrs Brian Clough, a Clacton family
    since 1837

In memory of Alfred George Coker

Graham and Janice Dale, Holland-on-Sea

George Alexander Denham

Patrica Cockree

Mrs Julie Dowler

In memory of Andrew Eaton, Clacton-on-Sea

John and Jennifer Elsom, Holland-on-Sea

Rodney Fissler, Clacton-on-Sea

Dave and Rita Gant, Clacton-on-Sea

Bob Grimwood

To Mark, 25 years in Clacton, Stephen Hackett

Mrs B W Harper

Paul Heather

Peter Hogg

The Horrell Family, Clacton-on-Sea

Golden Wedding 2008, Sheila and Barry Howe

In memory of Horace and Maud Howlett

Peter Antony Hutton

In memory of George and Kate Ingram

Gillian Jarvis

To my dearest Jeane, love Joan

In memory of a dear father and husband,
    Alfred John Kay

Remembering Brian Keeling, wife Marion

Frederick Kidd

Gordon D Kilburn

Happy Birthday Leon, July 14th,
    love Ralph and Pam xx

A tribute to my wife and son,
    Ann and Tim Maloney

Janet Moore, Clacton-on-Sea

Mrs J Morgan, Clacton-on-Sea

The Mumford Family of Essex

The O'Donnell family, Clacton, Frinton

To B C and S Pearce, love Mum and Dad

Mr and Mrs Debra and Christopher Percival

G F Pickering

Lillien Points, Holland-on-Sea, for Norman

David A Powell

David Privett

Anthony Proctor, Weeley Heath

Michael Stephen Allen Rhodes

Jan Rodwell

John Rosier, Thorpe-Le-Soken, Best Dad

The Scrivener Family, Clacton-on-Sea

Anne Simcox

Mary Simcox-Ayres

Audrey Grace Smith

Tony Sykes

In memory of Nan and Grandad Tuff,
    from the Grandchildren

Mr and Mrs P R Underhay, Holland-on-Sea

Valerie, Paul and Adrian Morris, Clacton

As a tribute to my parents, Bob Welton

In memory of R H West, Clacton

Peter Westwood

Barbara and Ted Wright, Holland-on-Sea, Essex

# INDEX

# FRITH PRODUCTS & SERVICES

Francis Frith would doubtless be pleased to know that the pioneering publishing venture he started in 1860 still continues today. Over a hundred and forty years later, The Francis Frith Collection continues in the same innovative tradition and is now one of the foremost publishers of vintage photographs in the world. Some of the current activities include:

## INTERIOR DECORATION

Today Frith's photographs can be seen framed and as giant wall murals in thousands of pubs, restaurants, hotels, banks, retail stores and other public buildings throughout the country. In every case they enhance the unique local atmosphere of the places they depict and provide reminders of gentler days in an increasingly busy and frenetic world.

## PRODUCT PROMOTIONS

Frith products are used by many major companies to promote the sales of their own products or to reinforce their own history and heritage. Frith promotions have been used by Hovis bread, Courage beers, Scots Porage Oats, Colman's mustard, Cadbury's foods, Mellow Birds coffee, Dunhill pipe tobacco, Guinness, and Bulmer's Cider.

## GENEALOGY AND FAMILY HISTORY

As the interest in family history and roots grows world-wide, more and more people are turning to Frith's photographs of Great Britain for images of the towns, villages and streets where their ancestors lived; and, of course, photographs of the churches and chapels where their ancestors were christened, married and buried are an essential part of every genealogy tree and family album.

## FRITH PRODUCTS

All Frith photographs are available Framed or just as Mounted Prints and Posters (size 23 x 16 inches). These may be ordered from the address below. Other products available are- Address Books, Calendars, Jigsaws, Canvas Prints, Notelets and local and prestige books.

## THE INTERNET

Already ninety thousand Frith photographs can be viewed and purchased on the internet through the Frith websites and a myriad of partner sites.

For more detailed information on Frith companies and products, look at this site:
www.francisfrith.com

**See the complete list of Frith Books at: www.francisfrith.com**
This web site is regularly updated with the latest list of publications from The Francis Frith Collection. If you wish to buy books relating to another part of the country that your local bookshop does not stock, you may purchase on-line.

*For further information, trade, or author enquiries please contact us at the address below:*
**The Francis Frith Collection, Unit 6, Oakley Business Park, Wylye Road, Dinton, Wiltshire SP3 5EU.**
Tel: +44 (0)1722 716 376  Fax: +44 (0)1722 716 881  Email: sales@francisfrith.co.uk

See Frith products on the internet at www.francisfrith.com

# FREE PRINT OF YOUR CHOICE

**Mounted Print**
*Overall size 14 x 11 inches (355 x 280mm)*

**Choose any Frith photograph in this book.**
Simply complete the Voucher opposite and return it with your remittance for £3.50 (to cover postage and handling) and we will print the photograph of your choice in SEPIA (size 11 x 8 inches) and supply it in a cream mount with a burgundy rule line (overall size 14 x 11 inches).
**Please note:** aerial photographs and photographs with a reference number starting with a "Z" are not Frith photographs and cannot be supplied under this offer. Offer valid for delivery to one UK address only.

**PLUS: Order additional Mounted Prints at HALF PRICE - £9.50 each** (normally £19.00)
If you would like to order more Frith prints from this book, possibly as gifts for friends and family, you can buy them at half price (with no additional postage and handling costs).

**PLUS: Have your Mounted Prints framed**
For an extra £18.00 per print you can have your mounted print(s) framed in an elegant polished wood and gilt moulding, overall size 16 x 13 inches (no additional postage and handling required).

---

**IMPORTANT!**

These special prices are only available if you use this form to order. You must use the ORIGINAL VOUCHER on this page (no copies permitted). We can only despatch to one UK address. This offer cannot be combined with any other offer.

---

*Send completed Voucher form to:*
**The Francis Frith Collection, Unit 6, Oakley Business Park, Wylye Road, Dinton, Wiltshire SP3 5EU**

# CHOOSE A PHOTOGRAPH FROM THIS BOOK

*Voucher* for **FREE** and Reduced Price Frith Prints

*Please do not photocopy this voucher. Only the original is valid, so please fill it in, cut it out and return it to us with your order.*

| Picture ref no | Page no | Qty | Mounted @ £9.50 | Framed + £18.00 | Total Cost £ |
|---|---|---|---|---|---|
| | | 1 | Free of charge* | £ | £ |
| | | | £9.50 | £ | £ |
| | | | £9.50 | £ | £ |
| | | | £9.50 | £ | £ |
| | | | £9.50 | £ | £ |
| | | | £9.50 | £ | £ |

*Please allow 28 days for delivery. Offer available to one UK address only*

| | |
|---|---|
| * Post & handling | £3.50 |
| **Total Order Cost** | £ |

Title of this book . . . . . . . . . . . . . . . . . . . . . . . . . . . . . .

I enclose a cheque/postal order for £ . . . . . . . . . .
made payable to 'The Francis Frith Collection'

OR please debit my Mastercard / Visa / Maestro card, details below

Card Number:

Issue No (Maestro only):          Valid from (Maestro):

Card Security Number:          Expires:

Signature:

Name Mr/Mrs/Ms . . . . . . . . . . . . . . . . . . . . . . . . . . . . . . . . .
Address . . . . . . . . . . . . . . . . . . . . . . . . . . . . . . . . . . . . . . . .
. . . . . . . . . . . . . . . . . . . . . . . . . . . . . . . . . . . . . . . . . . . . . .
. . . . . . . . . . . . . . . . . . . . . . . . . . . . . . . . . . . . . . . . . . . . . .
. . . . . . . . . . . . . . . . . . . . . . . . . . Postcode . . . . . . . . . . . .
Daytime Tel No . . . . . . . . . . . . . . . . . . . . . . . . . . . . . . . . . .
Email . . . . . . . . . . . . . . . . . . . . . . . . . . . . . . . . . . . . . . . . .

Valid to 31/12/12

**Free Print – see overleaf**

## Can you help us with information about any of the Frith photographs in this book?

We are gradually compiling an historical record for each of the photographs in the Frith archive. It is always fascinating to find out the names of the people shown in the pictures, as well as insights into the shops, buildings and other features depicted.

If you recognize anyone in the photographs in this book, or if you have information not already included in the author's caption, do let us know. We would love to hear from you, and will try to publish it in future books or articles.

## An Invitation from The Francis Frith Collection to Share Your Memories

The 'Share Your Memories' feature of our website allows members of the public to add personal memories relating to the places featured in our photographs, or comment on others already added. Seeing a place from your past can rekindle forgotten or long held memories. Why not visit the website, find photographs of places you know well and add YOUR story for others to read and enjoy? We would love to hear from you!

**www.francisfrith.com/memories**

## Our production team

Frith books are produced by a small dedicated team at offices near Salisbury. Most have worked with the Frith Collection for many years. All have in common one quality: they have a passion for the Frith Collection.

## Frith Books and Gifts

We have a wide range of books and gifts available on our website utilising our photographic archive, many of which can be individually personalised.

**www.francisfrith.com**